Masters of Spinjitzu

NINJA VS. THE OVERLORD

WRITTEN BY
CLAIRE SIPI

OUTWIT THE OVERLORD

SEASON TWO of NINJAGO®: Masters of Spinjitzu sees the ninja, joined by Green Ninja Lloyd, thwart Lord Garmadon—only for him to rise again! But evil Garmadon has not returned alone. A devious entity called the Overlord and his dangerous Stone Army have arrived. In Season Three, the Overlord returns to threaten New Ninjago City with an army of robotic Nindroids. The Ninja must use an arsenal of high-tech weapons to fight back.

HOW TO USE THIS BOOK

This book is a guideto the LEGO® NINJAGO® minifigures of Seasons 2 and 3. Learn all about the Ninja's awsome new skills and weapons, and how they use them to battle the fiendish Overlord.

To find out more about this minifigure see p.23.

CONTENTS

KIMONO KAI

ELEMENTAL FIRE NINJA

NINJA FILE

LIKES: His Fire Mech
DISLIKES: Fighting evil Nya
FRIENDS: Kimono ninja
FOES: Greedy Overlords
SKILLS: Fighting off Garmadon's scouts
GEAR: Elemental Fire Blade

SET NAME: Kai's Fire Mech
SET NUMBER: 70500
YEAR: 2013

DID YOU KNOW?

This version of Kai, wearing his elemental robes, is quite rare, as it can only be found in Kai's Fire Mech (set 70500).

Warrior head wrap with gold three-point crown visor

Elemental kimono with sash complete with fire symbol on the back

MAJOR FIREPOWER!

The awesome Fire Mech's huge robot form has impenetrable armor, cannons, katana swords, and serrated blades. Kai pilots it from a cockpit at the top.

Double-edged elemental Blade of Fire

IN THE TEMPLE OF LIGHT, fiery Kai gets his elemental powers back and his new kimono-style robe reflects the powerful energy now coursing through him. Red-hot Kai is ready to fight the Overlord's Stone Warriors in his mighty Fire Mech, in a titanic battle for control of the four elemental blades.

KIMONO JAY
ELEMENTAL LIGHTNING NINJA

NINJA FILE

LIKES: Fiery rocket pack
DISLIKES: Fast missiles
FRIENDS: Kimono ninja
FOES: General Kozu
SKILLS: Escaping the Warrior Bike
GEAR: Elemental Lightning Blade

SET NAME: Warrior Bike
SET NUMBER: 70501
YEAR: 2013

Elemental kimono with sash and lightning symbol on the back

Elemental Lightning Blade

TEMPLE OF LIGHT TRANSFORMATION

When Lloyd strikes the bell in the Temple of Light, the energy produced raises the ninja to a higher elemental status. Jay regains his power over lightning and his sword manifests a blade representing this element.

DID YOU KNOW?

Jay uses a jet pack to escape from the Stone Warrior, who is in hot pursuit on his Warrior Bike (set 70501).

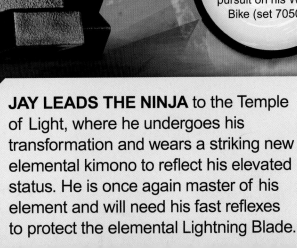

JAY LEADS THE NINJA to the Temple of Light, where he undergoes his transformation and wears a striking new elemental kimono to reflect his elevated status. He is once again master of his element and will need his fast reflexes to protect the elemental Lightning Blade.

KIMONO COLE

ELEMENTAL EARTH NINJA

NINJA FILE

LIKES: Defeating the Stone Warriors
DISLIKES: Losing his elemental Earth Blade
FRIENDS: Kimono ninja
FOES: Stone Swordsman
SKILLS: Deadly drilling
GEAR: Elemental Earth Blade

SET NAME: Cole's Earth Driller
SET NUMBER: 70502
YEAR: 2013

Ninja head wrap protects Cole's identity

Kimono in shades of Cole's trademark black colour

COLE'S EARTH DRILLER

This super-tough armored vehicle has a powerful rotating drill piece and can plough its way through any obstacle—including stone! With Cole in the driving seat, the ninja use these wheels to escape from the Stone Army.

Spinning drill piece

AFTER HAVING LOST but then regained his powers, Cole can't wait to take charge and see off the Stone Warriors. His sleek new kimono-style outfit is perfect for the job. Wielding the Earth Blade and harnessing his element, Cole is a force to be reckoned with. He has never been stronger.

KIMONO ZANE
ELEMENTAL ICE NINJA

Elemental Ice Blade

Elemental kimono with sash and ice symbol on the back

DID YOU KNOW?

Zane's elemental blade can generate frost and ice. It can fire freezing bolts and freeze things in place.

FALCON FRIEND

Zane's robot falcon was created by Zane's father, Dr. Julien, and first appears in LEGO® form in set 70724. It shares a special bond with Zane and can communicate with him in his dreams. The Stone Army captures it, but Zane soon stealthily swoops to the rescue!

ZANE'S NEWLY ENHANCED POWERS are as cool and icy as his new kimono-style ninja outfit. Armed with the double-edged Ice Blade, Zane is ready to freeze out the enemy—and he is able to produce an icy tornado powerful enough to knock even the Stone Warriors out cold!

LORD GARMADON

DARK ISLAND MASTER

NINJA FILE

LIKES: Giving orders
DISLIKES: Light
FRIENDS: General Kozu
FOES: The Green Ninja
SKILLS: Managing the unruly Stone Army
GEAR: Mega-Weapon

SET NAME: Temple of Light
SET NUMBER: 70505
YEAR: 2013

Helmet of Shadows shows the Stone Army's scorpion claw symbol.

Removable second torso with two extra arms

ISLAND OF DARKNESS
When Lord Garmadon reads about the Island of Darkness in Captain Soto's log, he is determined to find this evil place.

THE FORMIDABLE Master of Darkness has not given up on his evil scheme to take over Ninjago Island. Under the guidance of the sinister Overlord, and looking more evil than ever, Lord Garmadon has revenge on his mind. He takes control of the Stone Army on the Island of Darkness, ready to attack.

OVERLORD

GOLDEN MASTER

LIKES: Inflicting pain, ruling Ninjago Island
DISLIKES: Losing a fight
FRIENDS: Overlords don't need friends
FOES: Everyone
SKILLS: Creating Stone Armies, flying
GEAR: Garmatron

SET NAME: Battle for Ninjago City
SET NUMBER: 70728
YEAR: 2014

Full helmet with cheek guards

Spiked shoulder armor

Serrated blade weapon with red ax head

The Overlord is the only LEGO NINJAGO minifigure to wear a skirt piece.

THE DARK FALL OF NINJAGO ISLAND

In a combined attack, Lord Garmadon fires Dark Matter over the land, disrupting the balance between good and evil. It also allows the Overlord to escape while darkness infects the citizens.

FOR MANY YEARS nobody knew what the Overlord looked like in physical minifigure form. He had been spotted only as a dark shadow—trying to defeat goodness and bring evil to the world. Here he appears in his Golden Master form, proving this Overlord is a sinister shapeshifter!

GENERAL KOZU

STONE-FACED LEADER

Samurai-style helmet features Stone Army decoration

Unique torso extension piece gives Kozu his extra arms

DID YOU KNOW?

The Stone Army soldiers speak a mysterious language of their own. General Kozu acts as their translator.

THE ULTIMATE WEAPON

The Garmatron—a caterpillar-tracked battle machine—can push aside anything in its path. Armed with a front cannon and side turrets to fire missiles, Kozu feels on top of the world from the driving seat.

Stone-grey detailing covers Kozu's belt, legs, and torso.

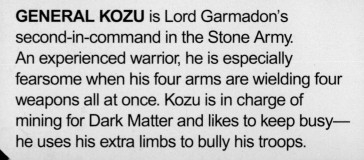

GENERAL KOZU is Lord Garmadon's second-in-command in the Stone Army. An experienced warrior, he is especially fearsome when his four arms are wielding four weapons all at once. Kozu is in charge of mining for Dark Matter and likes to keep busy—he uses his extra limbs to bully his troops.

STONE ARMY WARRIOR
UNDERWORLD SOLDIER ON THE UP

NINJA FILE

LIKES: Following orders
DISLIKES: Obstacles in his path to destruction
FRIENDS: Stone Warriors
FOES: Anyone "good"
SKILLS: Swordplay
GEAR: Butterfly sword, katana

SET NAME: Warrior Bike, The Golden Dragon
SET NUMBER: 70501, 70503
YEAR: 2013

As befits his rank, the warrior wears a winged helmet similar to Kozu's.

Ridged shoulder armor is common for Stone Army warriors and swordsmen.

The warrior wields his butterfly sword in one hand and his katana in the other.

FORCES OF DARKNESS

Originally created to defeat the First Spinjitzu Master and destroy all goodness in the land, the Stone Army is back in full force. The troops begin their mission massed on the Island of Darkness, waiting for their orders to roll out and take over Ninjago Island.

WHEN THE STONE ARMY was created by the Overlord, this tough warrior was built out of indestructible stone from the Underworld. Like his fellow soldiers, he is a tough-as-rock battle machine. He is rigidly unbending in his obedience, always follows orders and would love to crush the ninja.

GOLDEN NINJA
ULTIMATE SPINJITZU MASTER

NINJA FILE

LIKES: Defending Ninjago
DISLIKES: Catapults
FRIENDS: Golden Dragon
FOES: The Overlord
SKILLS: Summoning the Golden Dragon
GEAR: Golden Mech Sword

SET NAME: The Golden Dragon, Temple of Light
SET NUMBER: 70503, 70505
YEAR: 2013

Golden robes have the same pattern as one of his Green Ninja variants.

Even Lloyd's face and hands become gold when he harnesses the Golden Power!

DID YOU KNOW?
The Golden Power is a combination of all the main Elements of Ninjago: fire, earth, lightning, ice, and energy.

THE GOLDEN TOUCH
This ancient fighting Mech will only respond to the Golden Ninja's powers. Alongside the Golden Dragon, Lloyd finds it and awakens it in the Temple of Light.

Lloyd's seat in the cockpit is shaded by an oversized golden conical hat.

LLOYD GARMADON becomes the Golden Ninja after his first battle with the Overlord. He is now the most powerful ninja of all. His shimmering golden robe and armor are symbolic of his status and his potential to harness the Golden Power. With this upgrade he can overthrow the Overlord!

GOLDEN DRAGON
LEGENDARY SPINJITZU CREATURE

NINJA FILE

LIKES: Flying into battle
DISLIKES: Evil minions
FRIENDS: Master Lloyd
FOES: The Stone Army
SKILLS: Bellowing fire
GEAR: Dragon sphere

SET NAME: The Golden Dragon
SET NUMBER: 70503
YEAR: 2013

Lloyd rides the Golden Dragon from a white saddle flanked by flags.

Jaws can open wide to release sphere missile

DRAGON POWER!
Equipped with a cannon within its jaws, the magnificent Golden Dragon can fire dragon sphere missiles at the enemy! This dragon is a formidable battle machine, with huge extendable wings shaped like razor-sharp claws.

Head mold is the same as Cole's Earth Dragon, but painted gold with distinct green markings.

Long golden blade pieces uniquely used for fannable wings

AS THE GOLDEN NINJA, Lloyd uses his Golden Power to summon the mighty and mysterious Golden Dragon to battle by his side. He harnesses the creature's powers at the Temple of Light, and together, with their powers combined, they drive away the Stone Army and defeat the Overlord.

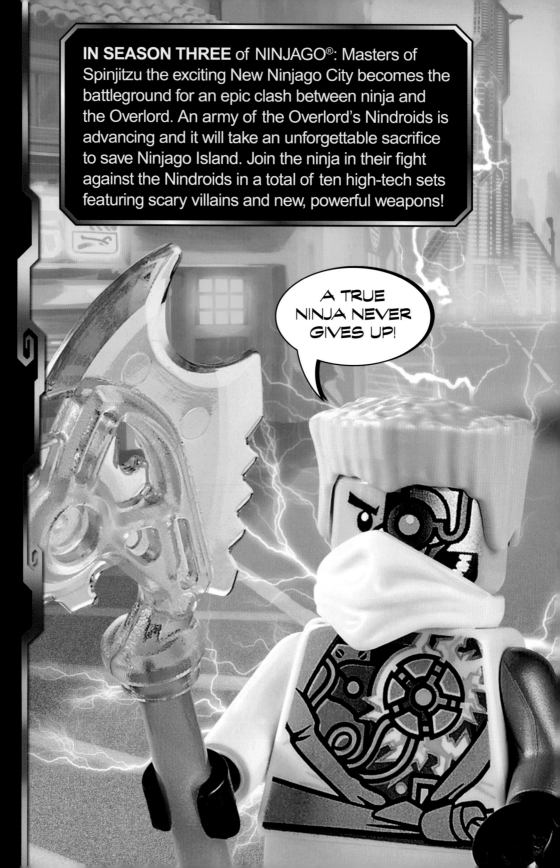

IN SEASON THREE of NINJAGO®: Masters of Spinjitzu the exciting New Ninjago City becomes the battleground for an epic clash between ninja and the Overlord. An army of the Overlord's Nindroids is advancing and it will take an unforgettable sacrifice to save Ninjago Island. Join the ninja in their fight against the Nindroids in a total of ten high-tech sets featuring scary villains and new, powerful weapons!

A TRUE NINJA NEVER GIVES UP!

NINJA VS. THE OVERLORD AND HIS NINDROIDS

MASTER GARMADON
SPINJITZU MASTER REBORN

Simple bo staff used for berating students, not fighting.

Garmadon's evil activities have turned his hair gray.

NINJA FILE

LIKES: Being good again
DISLIKES: His evil past
FRIENDS: Brother Wu
FOES: Digital Overlord
SKILLS: Teaching ninja
GEAR: Bo staff

SET NAME: Nindroid Mech Dragon
SET NUMBER: 70725
YEAR: 2014

Flowing robes decorated with a golden clasp and ancient writings

NINJA MENTOR
Dressed in variant robes from Ninja DBX (set 70750), Master Garmadon enjoys teaching the Art of the Silent Fist—a martial arts style involving misdirection and avoiding enemy attacks.

A tear in the back of the robes reveals a purple snake tattoo.

COMPLETELY PURIFIED of evil, Garmadon transforms back into a man when the Overlord is seemingly defeated by Lloyd, the Golden Ninja. His extra arms and dark-lord armor disappear, along with the dark magic that possessed him, to be replaced by the ninja robes of a peace-loving Spinjitzu Master.

THE OVERBORG

POSSESSED COMPUTER GENIUS

NINJA FILE

LIKES: Inventing gadgets
DISLIKES: Being controlled like a machine
FRIENDS: Techno Zane
FOES: The Overlord
SKILLS: Chasing
GEAR: Katana, saw

SET NAME: OverBorg Attack
SET NUMBER: 70722
YEAR: 2014

Dual-sided head shows Cyrus Borg has not gone for good.

Hairpiece with robotic parts and cybernetic eyepiece

Saw-bladed weapon is common amongst the Nindroids.

A spider-legged mech transports the OverBorg around Ninjago.

TOWN PLANNER
After the first defeat of the Overlord, Cyrus Borg strove to make Ninjago Island a center of technological advancement. He rebuilt Ninjago City and named it "New Ninjago City."

CYRUS BORG is an inventor, computer genius, and upstanding Ninjago citizen. But a bite from Pythor turns him into a cyber robot, controlled by the now-digital Overlord. Transformed into OverBorg, he uses his technological skills to summon the Nindroid Army in an attempt to rule Ninjago Island.

TECHNO COLE
REBOOTED EARTH NINJA

NINJA FILE

LIKES: New technology
DISLIKES: Hover Hunters
FRIENDS: Techno ninja
FOES: General Cryptor
SKILLS: Converting Security
Mechs into Earth Mechs
GEAR: Green Techno-Blade

SET NAME: Hover Hunter,
Thunder Raider
SET NUMBER: 70720,
70723
YEAR: 2014

This is one of only two Cole minifigures to show his hair.

Cole's Techno-Blade resembles a set of nunchuks.

DID YOU KNOW?
The Techno-Blades can hack into computer systems and transform ordinary machinery into awesome hi-tech ninja vehicles.

COLE'S EARTH MECH
Cole pilots his Earth Mech from a small cockpit at the top of the huge robot, and fires missiles at his foes from the sword blasters on its arms.

High-powered sword blaster

DRESSED IN HIS STYLISH black Techno robes, with a matching bandana to help block facial-recognition software, Cole is ready to battle this latest enemy, the Nindroids. He loves a challenge and will push his ninja skills to their limits using the new techno gear—including his chained Techno-Blade.

TECHNO KAI
REBOOTED FIRE NINJA

NINJA FILE

LIKES: Transforming cars into weapons
DISLIKES: Insects
FRIENDS: Techno ninja
FOES: General Cryptor
SKILLS: Aiming missiles
GEAR: Red Techno-Blade

SET NAME: Kai Fighter, Ninja Charger
SET NUMBER: 70721, 70727
YEAR: 2014

Bandana disrupts facial-recognition software

Scarlet Techno-Blade

Techno robes with printed flame design

DID YOU KNOW?

Kai's X-1 Ninja Charger vehicle also has a built-in Recon Nindroid with jagged blades for aerial battle.

ON THE CHARGE

Watch out Nindroids! In his awesome X-1 Ninja Charger, Kai is a formidable opponent. This super car is decked out with missiles and a dual shooter in the central engine bay. Lift the hood to activate the built-in interceptor bike.

KAI'S FLAMING TECHNO SUIT complements his fiery fighting style. He wears a matching red bandana to hide his face, but his hair is uncovered, like all of the Techno ninja. With his new sword-like Techno-Blade, Kai will channel all his strength to fight the sinister Nindroid Army.

TECHNO JAY
REBOOTED LIGHTNING NINJA

Each Techno-Blade is a different color—Jay's is lightning yellow.

NINJA FILE

LIKES: His off-roader
DISLIKES: The Nindroid's double laser cannon
FRIENDS: Techno ninja
FOES: Nindroids
SKILLS: Maneuvering the Thunder Raider
GEAR: Yellow Techno-Blade

SET NAME: Thunder Raider
SET NUMBER: 70723
YEAR: 2014

DID YOU KNOW?
Jay falls out with Cole when he discovers that Nya has feelings for the Earth Ninja as well as him.

New robe design, featuring streaks of lightning

THUNDER AND LIGHTNING
Jay's super-fast off-roader is a highly versatile ninja vehicle. The high-grip front tank treads and huge rear wheels power effortlessly over rough terrain at high speed.

In attack mode, the Thunder Raider fires hidden missiles.

JAY CAN MOVE at lightning speed, so his new Techno robes are extra mobile and decorated with electric-blue streaks of lightning. Just as quick with his brain, creative Jay always knows how to use his chainsaw Techno-Blade to its full effect. Go, ninja!

TECHNO ZANE

ROBOTIC NINJA OF ICE

This Techno robe variant includes pauldrons and crossed sashes.

NINJA FILE

LIKES: Flying his glider
DISLIKES: Nindroids
FRIENDS: P.I.X.A.L.
FOES: Nindroid army
SKILLS: Piloting
GEAR: Techno-Blade and shield, katana blades

SET NAME: Battle for Ninjago City
SET NUMBER: 70728
YEAR: 2014

To fight the Nindroids, Zane wields a blue Techno-Blade.

BATTLE-SCARRED

During battle with the Nindroids, in NinjaCopter (set 70724), Zane is badly damaged—seemingly beyond repair. But in Destructoid (set 70726), he appears rebooted, with his robotic parts hidden again!

LEARNING ABOUT HIS PAST only helps to make Zane a better ninja. Having reached his full potential, he is quick to locate his Techno-Blade—and even quicker to use it against the invading Nindroids. However, will he be strong enough to return after he is injured in battle?

TECHNO LLOYD
REBOOTED GREEN NINJA

Golden shoulder armor with scabbard for two katanas

DID YOU KNOW?
Lloyd's Techno suit is a mixture of all four of his previous ninja suits, with green legs and gold armor.

NINJA FILE

LIKES: Riding his Ninja Cycle
DISLIKES: Retreating
FRIENDS: His father—Master Garmadon
FOES: The OverBorg
SKILLS: Crushing Nindroids with his bike
GEAR: Golden swords

SET NAME: OverBorg Attack
SET NUMBER: 70722
YEAR: 2014

Techno suit with Golden Power emblem front and back

GREEN NINJA CYCLE
Zooming around on his Ninja Cycle, Techno Lloyd becomes a green and gold blur. The Overborg won't be able to catch him on this super slick machine.

Green and gold color scheme to match Lloyd's robes

THE GREEN NINJA is more powerful than ever and master of his Golden Power. His new Techno suit is emblazoned front and back with the Golden Power emblem, proudly showing off his elevated ninja status. With his golden armor and weapons, Techno Lloyd is primed for battle with the Overlord.

SAMURAI X
PHOENIX FLAME WARRIOR

Samurai helmet with ornamental spiked crest

Silver katana helps in fighting evil Nindroids

All-new armor with phoenix emblem

NINJA FILE

LIKES: Defeating Nindroids
DISLIKES: Spidery OverBorg. Two legs are enough on a villain!
FRIENDS: Kind Zane
FOES: Evil Tech Wu
SKILLS: Guarding ninja
GEAR: Ninja swords

SET NAME: Battle for Ninjago City
SET NUMBER: 70728
YEAR: 2014

DID YOU KNOW?
Nya's helmet and face mask were new molds, created for Nya's 2012 Samurai X armor.

SAMURAI VS. NINDROIDS
Disguised as the mysterious warrior Samurai X, Nya shows the Nindroids what an accomplished and fierce fighter she is with her stealthy samurai moves!

NOT MANY PEOPLE know of Nya's secret identity. This smart girl is not only a superb engineer, but a skilled sword fighter too! She becomes Samurai X so she can fight alongside the boys, and her elaborate samurai armor and crested helmet reflect her warrior status.

TECHNO WU
GOOD MASTER GONE BAD

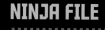

Traditional conical hat now looks like it is made out of metal, not bamboo.

Evil, red robot eyes

Black and white robe displays cyber robot parts.

NINJA FILE

LIKES: Flying the MechDragon
DISLIKES: Ninja escaping in Nya's car
FRIENDS: Pythor
FOES: All his old friends
SKILLS: Battling Garmadon
GEAR: Black bo staff

SET NAME: Nindroid MechDragon
SET NUMBER: 70725
YEAR: 2014

VICTIM OF THE OVERLORD
The Overlord probes Master Wu's memory to find out where the ninja are hiding. He then turns Wu into his latest cyber drone victim—Techno Wu—and forces him to attack the ninja and Garmadon. This is a battle the ninja don't want to have to fight.

GONE ARE THE white kimono and beard of a kind teacher—poor Master Wu has been captured by the Overlord and transformed into an evil robot. In this variant he wears black, befitting of his new dark status. Have the ninja lost their beloved master forever?

P.I.X.A.L.
ACE ANDROID

The other side of P.I.X.A.L.'s face reveals a scowl and red eyes to show that she is under the Overlord's control.

NINJA FILE

LIKES: Puzzles
DISLIKES: Nindroids
FRIENDS: Zane
FOES: Digital Overlord
SKILLS: Using technology
GEAR: Spike blade

SET NAME: NinjaCopter
SET NUMBER: 70724
YEAR: 2014

Spike blade is similar to the saw blades commonly used by Nindroids.

FRIENDS FOR LIFE

P.I.X.A.L. changes from cold and mechanical to loyal friend when Zane uses his Techno-Blade to hack her programming. They go on to destroy many Nindroids together. When Zane is hurt, the two discover they are compatible and merge into one being—a move that saves Zane's life!

AS AN ANDROID, P.I.X.A.L. (Primary Interactive X-ternal Assistant Life-form) is a robot. While under the control of the Digital Overlord, she copies Zane's mechanisms to make the Nindroid Army. But she is eventually freed from her programming and changes her ways.

GENERAL CRYPTOR

LEADER OF THE NINDROID ARMY

Ninja wrap with attached robot eye piece

Ground-to-air laser rocket launcher

Sinister red buttons for firing lasers

NINJA FILE

LIKES: Blabbering
DISLIKES: Getting kicked
FRIENDS: Nindroid Army
FOES: Kai and the ninja
SKILLS: Firing laser beams
GEAR: Laser rocket launcher, bazooka

SET NAME: Kai's Fighter, Nindroid MechDragon, Destructoid
SET NUMBER: 70721, 70725, 70726
YEAR: 2014

DESTRUCTIVE DESTRUCTOID

General Cryptor controls his battle tank from its 360-degree rotating command center. He unleashes lasers and missiles from the disc shooter and uses the razor-sharp chopping blades to attack the enemy.

SECOND-IN-COMMAND to the Overlord, the talkative and quick-tempered General Cryptor is the most powerful and advanced of the Nindroids, reflected by his unique armor. Cryptor believes himself to be the greatest warrior in the world and tends to severely underestimate his enemies!

NINDROID WARRIOR
HIGH-TECH FIGHTING MACHINE

NINJA FILE

LIKES: Nindroid Jet Fighter
DISLIKES: Getting captured
FRIENDS: Fellow warriors
FOES: Zane—the blueprint for the warrior's creation
SKILLS: Sharp aim
GEAR: Double laser blades

SET NAME: Thunder Raider, NinjaCopter, X-1 Ninja Charger, Battle for Ninjago City, Dareth vs. Nindroid (polybag)
SET NUMBER: 70723, 70724, 70727, 70728
YEAR: 2014

Kimono robe with exposed cyber robot parts

Double laser blades

AERIAL ATTACK
The Nindroid warrior from Nindroid MechDragon (set 70725), launches an air attack on the ninja wearing a jet pack and wielding an axe-chainsaw spear.

THE NINDROID WARRIOR is a mechanical soldier modeled on Zane's programming. This result is a stronger, faster and more agile fighter than Zane, but lacking in emotions. Its only mission is to fight the ninja and follow orders from its master, the Overlord.

DK | Penguin Random House

Project Editor Emma Grange
Senior Designers Jo Connor, Mark Penfound
Editors Arushi Vats, Rosie Peet, Matt Jones, Clare Millar
Designers Radhika Banerjee, Dimple Vohra,
Stefan Georgiou
Editorial Assistant Beth Davies
Pre-Production Producer Kavita Varma
Senior Producer Lloyd Robertson
Editorial Managers Paula Regan,
Chitra Subramanyam
Design Managers Guy Harvey, Jo Connor, Neha Ahuja
Creative Manager Sarah Harland
Publisher Julie Ferris
Art Director Lisa Lanzarini
Publishing Director Simon Beecroft

This edition published in 2017
First American Edition, 2016
Published in the United States by DK Publishing
345 Hudson Street, New York, New York 10014
DK, a Division of Penguin Random House LLC

Contains content previously published in LEGO®
NINJAGO® *Character Encyclopedia Updated and Expanded
Edition* (2016)

003–298874–Jul/17

Page design Copyright © 2017 Dorling Kindersley Limited

ISBN: 978-5-0010-1399-0
Printed in Heshan, China

ACKNOWLEDGEMENTS
DK would like to thank Randi Sørensen, Martin Leighton Lindhart,
Paul Hansford, Madeline Boushie, Simon Lucas, Nicolaas Johan Bernardo
Vás, and Daniel McKenna at the LEGO Group, Gary Ombler for extra
photography, Andy Jones for extra editorial help, Sam Bartlett for
design assistance and Claire Sipi for her writing. For the original edition
of this book, DK would like to thank Shari Last, Julia March,
Ruth Amos, Lauren Rosier, Mark Richards, Jon Hall,
Clive Savage, Ron Stobbart, and Catherine Saunders.

www.LEGO.com

www.dk.com
A WORLD OF IDEAS:
SEE ALL THERE IS TO KNOW